Xtreme Athletes

Apolo Ohno

Xtreme Athletes

Apolo Ohno

Ken Robison

MORGAN
REYNOLDS
PUBLISHING

Greensboro, North Carolina

Xtreme Athletes

Brock Lesnar
Apolo Ohno
Tito Ortiz
Danica Patrick
Michael Phelps
Kelly Slater
Michelle Wie
Shaun White

Xtreme Athletes: Apolo Ohno

Library of Congress Cataloging-in-Publication Data

Robison, Ken.
 Apolo Ohno / by Ken Robison.
   p. cm. -- (Xtreme athletes)
 Includes bibliographical references and index.
 ISBN 978-1-59935-186-5 (alk. paper) -- ISBN 978-1-59935-209-1
(e-book :alk. paper)
 1. Ohno, Apolo Anton--Juvenile literature. 2. Speed skaters--United
States--Biography--Juvenile literature. I. Title.
 GV850.O45R63 2012
 796.91'2092--dc22
 [B]

                                        2011014476

Printed in the United States of America
First Edition

Contents

one

The Cold, Wet Truth

Apolo Anton Ohno has won more Olympic medals than any other American speed skater. In the process he has become the sport's most famous face, showing up on television talk shows and at celebrity gatherings. But before he brought the excitement of short track speed skating into America's living rooms, before he created thousands of new fans for his sport, Apolo Ohno faced a crisis of confidence that nearly ended his career before it got started.

It was January of 1998, and Apolo was at a low point. He had just blown the

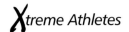

biggest opportunity of his young career and was wondering if he had what it takes to be the champion everyone expected him to be. To make things worse, he was alone. It was cold and rainy outside of the seaside cabin where he was staying by himself. Apolo had a big decision to make and no one to help him make it. That was unusual, because his father, Yuki, had always been there for him—driving him to swim meets and skating competitions, urging him to be better and better.

Apolo was just fifteen years old, and already he was one of the world's best short track skaters. But at the U.S. trials for the 1998 Olympics, he soon found out that he was still a kid among his more experienced adult competitors. He finished dead last and was so discouraged he told his father he wanted to quit.

Yuki Ohno knew his son better than anyone else did. He knew something drastic had to be done to restore Apolo's confidence and determination to fulfill his potential. So he drove Apolo back to their hometown in Federal Way, Washington, and then down to one of their favorite spots—Iron Springs Resort on the Pacific Coast south of Seattle. Father and son had spent a lot of time at the seaside resort in past years, walking along the beach and swimming during many summer trips. But this was winter, and this time Yuki Ohno didn't stay with Apolo. Yuki gave his son a difficult message when he left him at Iron Springs, "You have to do this alone, all by yourself in the cottage.

You have to take this path to come to the decision on your own."

For nine days the teenager lived by himself in the cabin. Nine days of running, riding a stationary bicycle, watching skating tapes, and thinking about his future. His sport did not offer much in the way of fame and riches. Was all the training, the pain, and the sacrifice worth it? As he ran, pedaled and pondered, Apolo Ohno found his answer. Finally, he called his father and said, "I want to skate."

Since that moment, Apolo Anton Ohno has become what his father knew he could be—America's No. 1 short track speed skater and the best-known face of his sport. His success on the ice track has brought Apolo fame as a champion of three Olympic Games. He has been cheered around the world by millions of fans who have watched on television as he won eight Olympic medals in 2002, 2006, and 2010. It has taken him to the bright lights of Hollywood, where he reached even more fans as a winner of *Dancing With the Stars.*

Through it all there has been one main person in Apolo's life—his father. Yuki Ohno has been in his son's corner through victory, defeat, injury, and controversy. "My father . . . is one of my heroes. And one of my partners in short track," Apolo said. "I'm a kid who used to never like being told what to do by anyone, but my dad has been my mentor and my guide."

Apolo and his father,
Yuki Ohno, in June 2010

two

Watch Out, Here He Comes

Federal Way is a suburban commuter town in the state of Washington, between Seattle and Tacoma. It is where Yuki raised Apolo after his mother left them when Apolo was just one-year-old.

Yuki Ohno was a son of a college administrator in Japan. His own father had left the family farm to pursue a career in education, and Yuki attended prestigious Japanese schools. He was expected to pursue an education at a prominent university. "They expected me to perform academically high," Yuki said. "It's the system over there. You've got to go the right channel from junior high and high school.

Tutoring, testing and entrance tests, but once you pass the entrance test for college, it doesn't matter who you are, you've got it made."

Yuki wasn't interested in that path. Instead, against his family's wishes, he came to America at eighteen years old. He worked at several jobs in Portland, Oregon, and Seattle—janitor, dishwasher, busboy, newspaper deliverer—and even studied accounting before deciding to enter beauty school. Yuki had an artistic touch, so he moved to London to study at the Vidal Sassoon school where he cut hair for fashion models. He eventually returned to Seattle and opened his own salon.

Yuki Ohno, then in his mid-thirties, met a teenaged American, Jerrie Lee, and they married in 1980. Apolo was born in May of 1982. Yuki chose to name his son Apolo after the Greek word *ap*, which means "to steer away from" and *lo*, which means "look out; here he comes." The message was clear: "Get out of the way. My son is coming."

When the marriage of Yuki and Jerrie ended in 1983, all of a sudden Yuki Ohno was a single dad of a one-year-old son. Throughout his career Apolo Ohno has had to answer questions about his mother. He responds by saying he has no contact with her and does not wish to have a relationship. "Because I was so young when my parents separated, I have no memories whatsoever of my mother," Ohno said. "Zero. Not of her holding me. Not of her being there with me. Not of her kissing me. Nothing. It's a void, an empty space. Moreover, because my personality is the way it is—and as well, I am who I am—I have no real desire to know her."

Ohno said he doesn't even know what his mother looked like. In a couple of photos that remain from those days, her face is hidden by shadows or poor lighting. And he doesn't know his mother's nationality. His father said Jerrie Lee was adopted but doesn't know much more than that. Apolo said:

> My father and I never talk about her because I have no interest in knowing her. It doesn't upset me and I'm not angry. I simply don't miss her because she isn't in my memory and it's hard to miss something you've never had. Maybe I would have turned out softer or less stubborn if I'd had a mom and been showered with affection. Then again, maybe I wouldn't have had the warrior instinct or the hunger to succeed. I never think of my mother. She was a biological donor and I'm grateful she carried me inside her for nine months. But she was never my mom.

During the 2002 Olympics, Apolo told an interviewer that after nineteen years it would be "strange" to meet his long-lost mother. "I don't have any [lost child] hotlines out for her," he said. In Vancouver for

the 2010 Winter Olympics, he again said he wanted no contact with his mother. His father is his parent, he insisted. "To be honest, at age 27, I don't even know if I'd recognize her. I don't know if I would have any connection. Since I can remember, I was raised by my father my entire life. So he's kind of been that mom and father figure, always."

Being a single father changed Yuki Ohno's life. His circle of hip friends from the hair fashion business dropped away. "Everything changed," Yuki said. "I had to change the diaper. I was completely out of the circle. Those people don't talk about kids." While his father worked at his salon, young Apolo often was left on his own, at day care or with friends. Yuki knew he needed to find something active for his energetic, independent son to get involved in. Yuki Ohno recalled thinking to himself, "Can I do this? I wasn't feeling confident at all. I was scared."

By the time Apolo was three years old, Yuki Ohno knew he had a gifted son. "I was a quick reader, musical and extremely agile," Apolo said. "Most of all, I picked things up very quickly. My dad felt he had a responsibility to help me live up to my potential and, as long as I could take it, push me to a higher level." That approach was evident when Yuki heard from a teacher that six-year-old Apolo wasn't focusing on his lessons. Apolo had walked away from his French lesson to read a book. "My dad figured out that I was bored and found a better school."

Sports seemed like the right fit for the energetic boy. Yuki had noticed his son showing natural athletic talent and a boldness that many kids did not, even in day care. When Yuki went one day to pick up Apolo, the three-year-old was at the top of the jungle gym. None of the adults could get him down.

When Apolo was five, his father bought him a small bicycle with training wheels. When he brought it home his father took the bike out of the trunk of his car and put it on the sidewalk, then turned around to get the training wheels. When he looked back up, Apolo was already on the bike and was riding away. His first time on a two-wheeler he wobbled a bit but didn't fall. He'd learned how to ride the bike from watching other people.

Apolo still remembers the first hill he ever rode down on his bike. "In the beginning my eyes were wide open with fear, but as I took off I felt the exhilaration of being in control and the speed

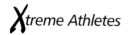

of flying. I remember the flash of green trees from the corner of my vision and hearing my father laughing"

Today, Apolo is deeply grateful for his father. "He saw something in me that I didn't see in myself," he says.

Apolo took up competitive swimming at age six. Once again, his father was there to make sure he got the proper training. During a practice at a public swimming program, Yuki noticed that Apolo was fooling around. So he took his son to a private swim club. Apolo saw the other kids at the private club had great technique. He jumped into the pool and began thrashing around. "Surprisingly, I kept up and the coach said I could stay. I learned all the strokes quickly and began to compete."

He also sang in a boys' chorus and took up in-line speed skating. Often his days would include morning swim practices, then school, then skating in the afternoon.

Apolo was extremely bright but also easily distracted. Yuki Ohno was concerned that Apolo's friends were leading him into activities that weren't good for him. Father and son often clashed as the young man sought greater freedom to party on weekends instead of traveling to athletic competitions. "I think there was probably a period of time where we would just fight a lot, just about anything," Apolo said. "It was mostly instigated by me, for sure." Later in his life, Apolo recognized that for what it was: a typical father-son relationship—a father trying to protect his son, son pushing him away.

On the athletic field, Apolo was competitive in everything he tried. At age twelve he won a Washington state championship swimming the breast stroke. He also won a number of in-line skating competitions. His father was beginning to see his son succeed in sports, just as he had predicted. "I had no doubt my son was going to excel at a very high level," Yuki said. "It took my best effort to channel his energy into sports and competition."

Apolo saw some of his friends in the racially mixed Federal Way neighborhood get into trouble. "A few of my friends made the choice to join the Bloods or the Crips (street gangs), but I never rolled that way. I never joined one because I was competing so much that I didn't feel the need—I got out my aggressions in the pool or skating rink." Although Yuki Ohno knew there was a risk his son could get caught up in that lifestyle, Apolo claimed his father never knew how bad some of the neighborhood kids were. "One guy was in the newspaper every week for the houses and cars he robbed. People got shot, people got stabbed—or went to jail."

Years later, during the 2010 Olympics, Apolo looked back at those days and said, "Sports saved me. I'm not sure what kind of trouble I would have gotten into, but I'm glad I never found out."

Federal Way, Apolo's Hometown

Federal Way is a city of nearly 90,000 residents in Washington state's King County. It lies along Puget Sound, twenty-five miles south of Seattle and eight miles north of Tacoma. Its location and proximity to Interstate 5 and several state highways makes it a desirable commute to Seattle and Tacoma as well as easy access to Sea-Tac airport.

Federal Way's Web site boasts "waterfront, lakes, green space and mountain views." Its weather is mild because of its proximity to Puget Sound and moist marine air. Temperatures average 75 degrees with .71 inches of precipitation in July and 33 degrees with 5.7 inches of precipitation in January.

The town was formed in the late 1800s as as a logging settlement. In the 1920s, Federal Highway 99 was built to link the town with Tacoma and Seattle. Federal Way High School was built in 1931

A view of Federal Way, Washington, from the Puget Sound shoreline

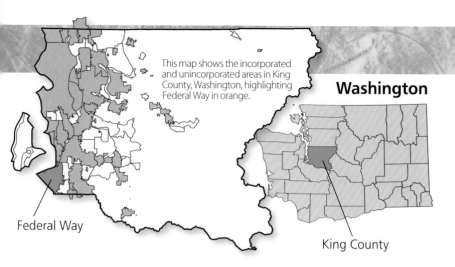

This map shows the incorporated and unincorporated areas in King County, Washington, highlighting Federal Way in orange.

Washington

Federal Way

King County

with money raised by selling land alongside Highway 99. The city was officially named Federal Way in the early 1950s. The city saw a housing boom in the '50s and '60s when homes were built for employees of Boeing and Weyerhaeuser. That spurred commercial growth, including SeaTac Mall in the 1970s.

The city reports that about 22,500 people are employed within the city limits with others commuting to Seattle, Tacoma, Kent, Auburn, Bellevue, and Sea Tac. The vast majority work in retail and service jobs.

The 2000 United State Census reported nearly 68 percent of Federal Way's 83,259 residents were twenty-one years old or older. The prominent racial demographics were white (69 percent), Asian (12 percent), African American (8 percent), and Hispanic/Latino (7.5 percent). Of the Asian population, more than 5 percent were Korean. ∎

three
Discovering The Ice

In 1994 Apolo and Yuki watched television coverage of the Winter Olympics in Lillehammer, Norway. Apolo was already a champion in-line skater and became captivated by short track speed skating. Yuki Ohno found a skating club in Eugene, Oregon. That was the start of Apolo Ohno's ice skating career. He also trained at the Puget Sound Hockey Center in Tacoma.

Eventually, they moved their training to Vancouver, an important city for ice skating in the Pacific Northwest. They would spend hours on the road, driving to training sessions and competitions. Soon Apolo began winning skating events in his age group. In January of 1996 he surprised everyone by finishing fourth at the Junior National Championships—quite a remarkable result for a thirteen-year-old with less than two years of experience.

That success drew interest from U.S. skating officials. Apolo was invited to the Olympic Training Center in Lake Placid, New York, to train with the U.S. Junior National Development Team. At fourteen, the Saghalie Junior High eighth-grader would be the youngest skater ever admitted to the center.

The invitation to train in Lake Placid also helped his father's bank account because his training would be funded by the national program. Yuki had

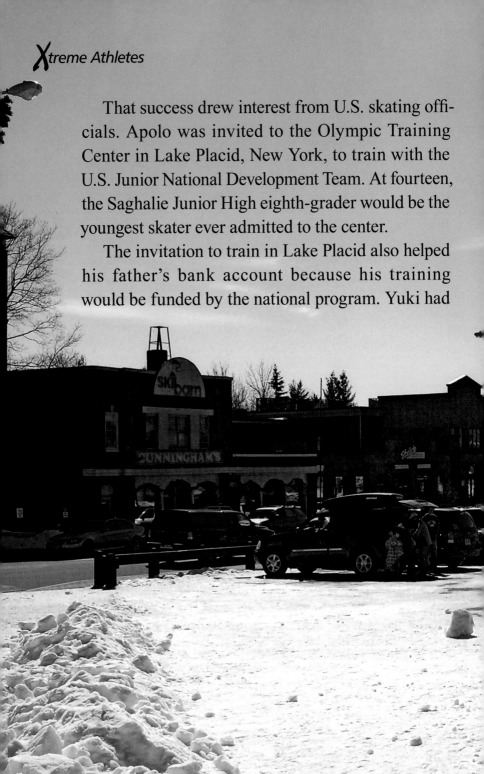

estimated he spent $2,000 a year in equipment alone and five hundred dollars in transportation and lodging every time Apolo competed. "I don't mind prioritizing expenses," Yuki said. "But there is a limit. We're getting close to that limit. I don't want to say to Apolo that we can't do some things, but we do need help."

The Olympic Center in Lake Placid, New York

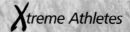

Speed Skating Equipment

Equipment worn by ice speed skaters are for protection and performance.

GLOVES: Sharp blades can cut skaters, so they wear gloves to protect their hands. Also, the skaters often place their hands on the ice to balance themselves as they lean into curves.

GOGGLES: Some skaters wear goggles to protect their eyes from cold wind and blowing ice. Tinted lenses can help reduce glare.

HELMETS: Because crashes are frequent, skaters wear helmets to protect their heads from hitting the ice or walls.

SKATES: The boots worn by short track skaters are made from heavy materials customized to stabilize the foot and ankle. They are designed to prevent injuries as skaters make sharp turns around corners.

The blades are not placed in the middle of the shoe. Instead, they are placed closer to the left side of the shoe so the boot does not come into contact with the ice as the skaters lean into their turns. ■

Apolo Ohno during the four lap men's short track trials on December 20, 2001, in Kearns, Utah

But Apolo didn't want to go to Lake Placid. He wanted to stay in Washington and hang out with friends at the Wild Waves water park in Federal Way. "He had his whole summer planned," Yuki said. "He was going to the water park and parties. That's all he wanted to do." Yuki was concerned Apolo might get into trouble with his friends in Federal Way. He felt his son was growing apart from him—and that his chance to be a world-class athlete might also be slipping away. "He was overprotective," Apolo said, "But I was getting in too much trouble back home, and it wasn't good." Yuki looked around and didn't want his son to follow the trends. He wanted Apolo to have a healthier lifestyle than simply staying up late, playing video games, and eating junk food like so many other teenagers.

When Apolo resisted going to Lake Placid, his father reminded him how important it was. Yuki believed the invitation was a ticket to being in the 1998 Olympics. Apolo wasn't sure. "Chances don't come around every day," Yuki said. "And if you don't grab them they never come back. Everyone gets one big opportunity, not four or five, because that's the only way life can be fair to each person." They fought for several months, but Yuki would not budge. In early June he packed Apolo's bags, drove him to the Seattle airport, handed him his ticket to Lake Placid, and dropped him off at the boarding gate.

But fourteen-year-old Apolo didn't get on the airplane. Instead, he called a friend to pick him up at the airport. Then he spent five days visiting malls and movie theaters and partying with friends.

It was the ultimate act of rebellion. "Dad told me, 'I know what's best for you. You need to listen,'" Ohno said. "He's from that Asian background, he's strict. But I'm 14, I don't want to do anything anybody says." Apolo said he had planned his mutiny all along. All he needed was a way out, and Yuki provided that. Apolo said:

> Dad literally packed my bags, put me in the car and drove me to the airport. The ride was silent and the tension was thick. If anger was a brick wall, I'd built a house around myself with barbed wire. Dad walked me to the terminal, got my ticket and took me to the boarding gate. Then he made a mistake . . . He said good-bye, told me I'd be OK, and left me to board the plane alone. I had never planned to get on that flight. For the next five days I went to fairs, the mall, parties and movies. I had a plan–I'd stay with each of my friends for a few days, then move on before their parents figured out anything was wrong and called my dad. I was 14, had no money, but I figured I could live that way for a year or more because I had friends

who lived all over Washington state. I was a kid trying to pull off the biggest act of rebellion in my life and I remember the exhilaration and the feeling that I was standing on the edge of a cliff, one foot in the air, about to step off.

For the next few days after his airport rebellion, Apolo would sneak home when Yuki was at work and get more clothes. He wasn't very secretive about his visits to his house. "As the days wore on, part of me was trying to get caught so I could have a final confrontation with my dad." Yuki was wise to his son's behavior, however. After discovering that Apolo never arrived in Lake Placid, Yuki let his son act out his rebellion for several days. Finally, afraid that Apolo was blowing his big chance, he tracked down the teenager at a friend's house and told him he had to come home.

Three days later Apolo returned home. For a week father and son worked to repair their relationship. Yuki told his son to remember what was most important in life. Apolo said:

Dad explained to me that no matter how tough a situation got, I could never again cut myself off from my family. 'Your friends may be with you a week, a month, a year, but in the end your family is the only thing that's permanent and I'm the one who will take care of you no matter what.' Still upset and angry, I knew deep down my father was right. I might no longer believe in the Boogeyman, but there were things that still scared me. Losing my father's love and support were at the top of the list.

A couple days later, father and son boarded an airplane together for the trip to Lake Placid. Yuki remembered that trip and said, "I escorted Apolo to Lake Placid. When I left, you could imagine the uncertainty. I didn't know if it was going to work out or not." Before he left the training center to return home, Yuki Ohno told the coaches, "Good luck if you think you can keep him here for three months."

A view of Lake Placid from
McKenzie Mountain in New York

four

A Teenager On Top

His first few weeks at Lake Placid, Apolo's unhappiness grew. He was far from his friends, and his new school was mostly white, quite a contrast from the racially diverse school back home. So that first month at the training center was a waste. Sometimes Apolo and another skater would drop out of the five-mile runs and go to Pizza Hut. "I hated it there," Apolo said. "I didn't talk to anybody. I didn't want anybody to help me. Then I thought, I'm having a good time, my dad's not here bossing me around, I'm young, and I can do whatever I want."

But what Apolo hated even more was his nickname—Chunky. That's what he was called by his fellow skaters because of his physique. "I was a thick kid," he said. "Strong but very thick." When he finished dead last in the training group's body fat test, Apolo told coach Pat Wentland, "I don't want to be

the fattest. I don't want to be the slowest. I want to be the best." From that moment on, Apolo embraced training with a new resolve. "He totally changed," Wentland said. "Every workout from then on, he had to win. I'd never seen that kind of turnaround so fast."

There was personal growth, also. Moving to Lake Placid was Ohno's first experience at living in a dorm with older skaters, without his father, and having to balance education and athletic training. "It has really helped him growing up with the kids here who have a direction and a goal," Wentland said. "They're all in bed by 9 p.m., watch what they eat. It's a huge change in lifestyle." Exactly the regimen Yuki Ohno knew his son needed.

Apolo thrived under Wentland's coaching. In 1997, at the age of fifteen, he won the U.S. Championship, putting him on the senior American team. It appeared he could be one of the top skaters at America's 1998 Olympic Trials.

But Apolo's teenaged rebellion and the attraction of his friends in Washington were still powerful. After finishing nineteenth overall at the 1997 World Championships, he returned to Seattle and quit training for several months. Ohno said:

Instead of putting focus on things I needed to do, I was messing around. I didn't dedicate myself. There was no want in my heart. I had no clue what it really took. I went through that summer and fall giving half the effort I had in me—if that much. I turned defiant; I mouthed off to coaches. I quit races. I quit competitions. I quit on myself and everyone around me. I simply didn't understand what it meant to be an Olympic athlete. And I didn't understand the rarity of the gift I had, an opportunity before me that you can't buy. I clearly had talent. And I was throwing it away.

By the time he showed up for the U.S. Olympic Trials back at Lake Placid in January of 1998, Apolo was out of shape and exhausted. He didn't want to be there. A favorite to make the team, he finished sixteenth in the field of sixteen, last place. Apolo had convinced himself he wouldn't succeed, and he had been right. It was hard for his father to watch. "The whole season was a mess," Yuki said. "He didn't know how to pace himself or how to take care of himself when he was traveling. At the Olympic trials he was completely exhausted. I had to watch while he was eaten alive. It was very bitter medicine for him to take. No. 1 to the very bottom."

It was such a devastating defeat, Wentland wondered if he'd ever see the young skater again. Apolo was fighting fear—that he might not be good enough.

If he didn't train and didn't care, he had an excuse. If he gave his best and still lost, would that be worse?

Discouraged and ready to quit the sport, Apolo went back home with his father. Yuki gave him a pep talk: if he didn't give skating a 100 percent effort, he'd always have regrets. That's when Yuki Ohno dropped Apolo off on the rainy beach resort at Iron Springs.

The rest of Apolo's career—the Olympic medals, the world titles, the international fame—are the result of those nine days of soul searching and his eventual decision to rededicate himself to his sport. "Everything had changed," he said. "My career had both ended and begun anew. I recognized that I

was talented and had a gift. I realized that I loved my sport."

Apolo knew he couldn't succeed by himself. He would need coaches, trainers, friends, and teammates. Most importantly, he would need the help of his true partner—his father. Apolo Ohno now understood what had been going on. "He had always been there, steering me from trouble, driving me to competitions, cheering from the stands, but I'd been unwilling to completely depend on his help." On the drive home from Iron Springs, Yuki Ohno's message was clear: he would be his son's partner as he trained for the 2002 Olympics.

Li Jiajun of China (center), Apolo Ohno (right), and Fabio Carta of Italy (left), turn a corner during their 500 meter final race at the World Short Track Speed Skating Championships in Sofia, Bulgaria, on March 20, 1999. Li took first place, Ohno placed second, and Carta finished third.

five

First Taste of Controversy

Apolo Ohno made the U.S. team as an alternate for the world championships in Vienna. While there, he made this entry in his journal:

> I am not going to mess up this time. When I go home, I really am going to be the different person I decided in Iron Springs I would be. I know what I want to do. I want to be the best I can be. I want to be the best in the world.

Apolo just kept getting better. That included being stronger mentally using confidence, focus, and relaxation techniques he learned from mental coach Dave Creswell and pain management techniques from sports psychologist Doug Jowdy.

He won three golds and a silver at the 1999 World Junior Championships in Montreal and a silver in the 500 meters in that year's World Championships in Sofia, Bulgaria, while battling chronic back pain.

But he had yet to find out how much jealousy and competitive anger were involved in the fast, dangerous sport of short track speed skating.

A panoramic view of downtown Montreal, Quebec

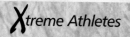

Short Track Skating

Short track ice skating dates back to the nineteenth century. As an indoor skating event, it differs in one important way from long track racing. In long track racing, skaters compete against a clock. In short track, on a tight 111 meters oval, they race against each other in a pack. This creates a strategy and skill that features some bumping and the potential for collisions and falls as skaters try to maneuver past each other to pass.

Short track skating began in Europe and eventually spread to the United States and Canada early in the twentieth century. The popularity of short track skating was helped by the North American rules, which included exciting mass starts. These rules were adopted for international competition at the Lake Placid Games in 1932. Because of the close quarters and the jostling of skaters, the walls of the rink are padded.

Short track skating was introduced to the Olympic Games in 1992 in Albertville, France, when four events were competed. The competition now includes eight events: men's and women's 500 meter; men's and women's 1000 meter; men's and women's 1500 meter; women's 3000 meter relay; and men's 5000 meter relay. ■

By 2001 Ohno had established himself as one of the world's best short track skaters. He won two golds and the overall silver at the World Championships and seemed to be peaking just in time for the U.S. Olympic Trials. But there were some challenges. He spent much of the summer and fall recovering from injuries. Then, two weeks before the trials, he and fellow American skater Shani Davis were shaken up when Ohno's car hit a patch of ice, went out of control, and flipped over several times. They kicked out the window and escaped, unhurt and feeling extremely lucky.

Back on the ice, Ohno dominated the Olympic trials in Utah. He won the 500 and 1500 meter and looked like a sure thing for the final race, the 1000 meter. But that race thrust Ohno into a major controversy that threatened his spot on the American team—and his reputation. Ohno was already assured of his place in the U.S. team, but his friend Shani Davis was not. Davis, in fact, had to win the 1000 meter to make the team.

Short track racing requires skating in tight quarters at fast speeds. Collisions and falls are common. Ohno understood that one slip could result in an injury that would end his Olympic chances. "Reporters asked me, 'Are you going to try to sweep?' I told them, 'No, I'm going to try to stay healthy and accomplish my goals. That's not one of them.'"

Not wanting to risk an injury that might keep him out of the upcoming Olympics, Ohno cruised at a safe pace in the 1000, finishing third behind Davis and Rusty Smith. As Davis crossed the finish line, Ohno was seen pumping his fist. He then gave his friend a

big hug. Those gestures suggested to some that Ohno had held back to let Shani win. Speed skating is an individual event. To determine the outcome of a race by letting a teammate win is a violation of the sport's code of conduct.

Apolo Ohno (right) looks at Shani Davis (left) during the men's 1000 meter short track trials in Kearns, Utah, on December 22, 2001.

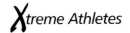

Tommy O'Hare, who lost his chance to make the team when Shani won, officially protested that Ohno and Smith had conspired to let Davis win. Witnesses claimed they overheard Ohno and Smith discussing the "fix." Ohno and Smith denied the charge and pointed out that none of the race officials had declared the race to be invalid. Ohno noted that the 1000 meter was Davis's best event and that Davis had set an American record in that event just a few months before the trials.

Ohno was hurt and angry that anyone would question his motives. The accusation was a serious hit to his reputation as a fair competitor. If the officials decided he had let Shani win he could be banned from competition. "I think Apolo is wondering why people are making statements that are untrue," his attorney Chris Cipoletti said. "I think he's holding up fairly well, but with any situation like this, it takes its toll."

Ohno has admitted he did not give 100 percent in the 1000 meter. He believed it was not necessary because he had already accomplished his goal of qualifying for all three events at the Olympics. What was most important, he said, was to stay away from injury. He explained his actions on that day:

> I went over to Shani after the race and congratulated him with a big smile and hug. It was an extremely natural reaction for me,

something I'd done to countless skaters in different races. I was glad Shani had done so well.
I felt I had too, skating safely and protecting my
place as a competitor for the Games. Someone
made a comment that since I showed such hap-
piness for Shani, it 'implied wrongdoing.' It
blows my mind that it's 'implied wrongdoing'
to be a good sport.

All the skaters testified to an arbitrator, who finally
ruled that there was no evidence to support O'Hare's
charge. But simply ending the controversy would
not be enough. Ohno's attorney, Cipoletti, asked
that the skaters' names be cleared. Arbitrator James
Holbrook issued a statement: "Neither Ohno, Smith
nor Davis violated the rules or code of conduct of
the U.S. Speedskating, USOC, or the International
Skating Union. . . . There is no evidence submitted
that would support any finding that the race had been
fixed." Once that dispute was settled, Ohno began
training for his first Olympics—amid more discus-
sion in the press about his role in the controversy during the trials. Little did he know that more controversy awaited in Salt Lake City.

The Olympic flame during
the 2002 Winter Games in
Salt Lake City, Utah

SIX

Apolo's First Olympics

The 2002 Olympic Games in Salt Lake City were Apolo Ohno's "coming out" party. In winning two medals—gold in the 1500 meter, silver in the 1000—he became an American winter sports hero. U.S. coach Pat Wentland had hoped that Ohno would help revive interest in short track skating. "It's a dying sport," Wentland said. "If Apolo scores big in Salt Lake and comes across as the personality he is, we finally have a shot to get noticed." Ohno grabbed attention for the sport but not in the way Wentland had in mind. Instead, Apolo's first competition in the Olympics was filled with drama and turned into an international incident.

Ohno's first Olympic final was in the 1000 meter, a race usually dominated by the Koreans. But defending Olympic champion Dong-Sung Kim had been knocked out in a semifinal, leaving Apolo as a favorite.

He grabbed the lead from Li Jiajun of China with two laps to go and still led with half a lap to go when chaos broke out. Jiajun tried to pass on the outside and bumped Apolo's arm. Huhn-Soo Ahn of Korea tried to pass on the inside but there was no room. The result was a crash that took down all three skaters and Canadian Mathieu Turcotte. Australia's Steven Bradbury, who had been skating safely in fifth place, passed the fallen skaters to win a most unlikely gold medal. But Apolo Ohno wasn't going to let a fall ruin his chances of earning his first Olympic medal. He scrambled and slid, feet first, across the finish line to claim the silver medal for second place.

What he didn't notice until a couple minutes later was a deep gash in his left thigh, caused by his own

Li Jiajun of China falls, clipping Apolo Ohno and causing a chain reaction crash of the leaders of the men's 1000 meter short track speed skating race at the Winter Olympics in Salt Lake City in February 2002. Next to Ohno are Hyun-soo Ahn of Korea and Mathieu Turcotte of Canada.

skate during the fall. It took six stitches to heal— a surgery done by former Olympic skating champion Eric Heiden, who was an on-site surgeon for the Salt Lake City Olympics. Ohno was wheeled to the podium in a wheelchair. He left the medal ceremony with two souvenirs of his first Olympic final—a silver medal and several stitches in his leg.

Later, while on crutches, Ohno had his typical positive outlook on the four-man crash that ended his hopes for gold. He called the race one of the best performances of his life. In a television interview the next night, Ohno told commentator Bob Costas: "That was definitely my time to shine. I was shining as bright as I could." Ohno said he believed he had the race won. "I was tasting it . . . going into the last

corner, that I was going to have the win under my belt. But this is short track and, you know, maybe it wasn't my day to win."

But the turmoil created by that race was just the first act. A few days later Ohno was involved in the major controversy of the 2002 Winter Olympics. In the 1500 meter—the longest of the short track races—Ohno waited in the back of the pack for several laps for a chance to move up. He found it with less than two laps to go, moving in to second place behind Kim. In the final lap Ohno attempted to pass Kim, but the Korean skater shifted to the inside to block him, a move called "cross tracking." Ohno raised his hands, a signal that he believed he was being blocked. (Cross tracking is

Apolo Ohno skates close on the heels of Dong-Sung Kim of South Korea during the men's 1,500 meter short track speed skating finals at the Winter Olympics in Salt Lake City, in 2002.

like cutting someone off in traffic. If a skater cuts in front of a rival to block his path, causing the other skater to slow down to avoid a collision, it is a "cross tracking" violation.)

Kim finished first in that race, ahead of Ohno. But the Korean skater was disqualified for blocking Ohno, who now had a gold medal. The decision by Olympic judges to disqualify Kim was met with mixed opinions. Some thought it was the correct call, others did not. Some blamed Ohno for influencing the officials with his "hands up" gesture.

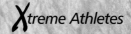
Rules Infractions

In short track speed skating, most infractions fall under two categories: bad skating and bad sportsmanship. Almost all of the infractions result in a disqualification.

Because skaters are moving fast, and closely together, even a small loss of concentration can cause bad skating to occur. Penalties usually happen when skaters are bumped or blocked—usually in an attempted pass.

Bad sportsmanship is rarer. It occurs when an infraction is intentional. If the sportsmanship infraction is severe, the skater can be disqualified.

The two most common infractions are "impeding" and "cross tracking." Other infractions, such as "kicking-out" and skating too slow are not as common. "Team skating" rarely is called.

IMPEDING: This occurs when one skater hinders another skater's progress—usually by bumping or pushing. Even a slight bump can disrupt another skater, throwing him off stride. He then must slow down to get back to his original balance and rhythm.

Skaters are not allowed to touch another skater, but it happens in tight quarters. The start of the 500 meter is especially crowded. Officials must decide whether a touch was intentional or if it impeded another skater's progress.

Sometimes one skater will block another skater from passing—often by slowing down or by sticking out his arm. This often occurs by accident, often when the impeding skater is trying to regain his balance.

Most of the time impeding is not done on purpose. If the official determines it was intentional and designed to injure the other skater, the impeding skater can be disqualified.

CROSS TRACKING: Skaters form "tracks" which are like lanes of traffic that they skate in. They are not marked, but the rules apply like traffic rules. As on a highway, skaters can change lanes, but are not allowed to cut off another skater.

The act of cutting off another skater is called cross tracking. When two skaters are close together and one moves into the other skater's "track," that is a cross tracking infraction. Skaters are allowed to change lanes, but they cannot do it in a way that causes another skater to slow down quickly to avoid falling.

KICKING OUT: Skate blades are sharp, and that makes them dangerous. If a skater's blades "kick out" from under him and interfere with another skater, that is an infraction. Sometimes when a skater is off-balance his skate will go out away from his body as he tries to regain his balance and is not intentional. Kicking out is only penalized when it is determined to be intentional or dangerous.

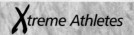

OFF TRACK: This is a "bad skating" violation, called when a skater goes inside the blocks on a turn. It is rare, and usually occurs when a skater loses track of the laps and thinks the race is over.

ASSISTANCE: When a skater helps another skater go faster or better. It is usually done by pushing the other skater to give him some added speed. It rarely occurs.

TEAM SKATING: When teammates scheme to ensure that one of them wins an individual race, it is an infraction. An intentional infraction can be called when a skater impedes another so his teammate can win. An infraction also can be called for "point manipulation" when team members control the outcome of a race to help a teammate gather more points for a better team result.

It is difficult to prove, and there are few guidelines for calling it. So it is rarely called and almost always controversial. What one person may see as team skating might simply be the normal course of a race.

SKATING TOO SLOW: There are two instances when this might be called. One usually occurs in the long 3,000 meter race when skaters—often tired from several days of skating—set a slow pace at the beginning. If the official deems the pace too slow, he can call for a restart. The other slow skating occurs when a skater cannot keep up with the pace. If a skater is lapped several times, the official can ask him to retire to the middle of the rink until the race is over. ■

The South Koreans were especially upset. They flooded the International Olympic Committee with e-mails and letters of protest. Some of the anger included death threats against Ohno. The harsh reaction from Koreans bothered Apolo. "I grew up around many Asian cultures, Korean one of them," he said. "A lot of my best friends were Korean growing up. I just didn't understand."

Perhaps the anger was understandable. The Koreans usually dominated short track speed skating, but so far in the 2002 Olympics they had come up empty in the 1000 meter and the 1500 meter and had been eliminated in the relay. Ohno later said he believed the resentment might be partly based on anti-American political sentiment in Korea.

The South Koreans appealed the race results, but the finish was upheld by both the Court of Arbitration for Sport and the International Olympic Committee.

A few days later Ohno's 2002 Olympics ended when he was disqualified in the 500 meter semifinals after he collided with Japanese skater Satoru Terao in the final lap. Ohno didn't fall down and finished third in the race. Even if he had not been disqualified, his third-place finish would have kept him out of the finals.

Ohno's 2002 Olympic success brought him his first taste of rock-star fame—quite a feat for an athlete in a sport that few people knew or understood

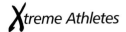

just a few months earlier. Even the athletes from such popular sports as snowboarding and freestyle skiing thought he was cool.

Ohno was on television talk shows and invited to Hollywood parties where he mingled with celebrities. In a visit to the White House, President George W. Bush said his staff had "Ohno-mania" during the Olympics. At another function, former President Bill Clinton asked Ohno for fashion advice on shoes. Ohno said:

> I went to an Oscar after-party, and I'm kicking it with the Backstreet Boys,

A Salt Lake City 2002
Winter Olympics medal

asking them, 'So, um, do you guys play sports?' I don't think they even realize they live in a different world. People wanted to know, 'What's your favorite suit, Armani or Versace?' I was like, 'Guys, I don't know. All I have is a Jordan jumpsuit.' But the attention was pretty cool.

It was a lot to handle for a teenager—even one as well-traveled and independent as Ohno. "I thought I was prepared for anything. But, the truth is, there's no way you can prepare yourself for that kind of thing. I mean, I was 19 years old. I was like, 'What's happening here? What's going on?' I never once in my life thought that short track would become that big, or that I would become . . . I don't know what. Some kind of symbol, I guess. It was so bizarre to be in the middle of that. It was borderline insanity."

These Olympic Games fueled Apolo Ohno's fire. He immediately began looking ahead to the 2006 Games. He moved back into the Olympic Training Center in Colorado Springs and began focusing on his skating. "The entire Olympic experience, the Olympic dream, the fact of being an Olympian—all of that was now in my blood, in my eyes, in everything about me," he said. "I felt the power of the Olympic spirit. And I wanted to train as if I had nothing, had no success. It's why I put my medals in my sock drawer instead

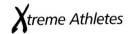

of on display. I wanted to act as if I had done nothing, had won nothing, yet."

But as Ohno put the Salt Lake City Olympics behind him, the Koreans could not. At the FIFA World Cup of soccer, two South Korean players mocked Ohno's "hands up" move after their team scored a goal against the U.S. team. In a poll taken before the World Cup, Ohno beat out Osama Bin Laden as the person Koreans did not want to attend the soccer event. Ohno did not participate in a 2003 speed skating meet in Korea for security reasons, but he still managed to win the World Cup in 2002-2003 and 2004-2005.

The next time Ohno showed up in South Korea was for the second event of the 2005 World Cup season. Dozens of riot police were on hand at Inchon Airport to assure his safety. They feared Koreans would still be resentful of the 2002 Olympics incident. But the authorities had nothing to fear. Ohno won two gold medals and the overall title. He also charmed the crowd by being accessible for interviews, cheering for Korean skaters, and embracing fans. "He won them over by being Apolo," said Jimmy Jang, former Korean national team coach who later coached Ohno. "The anger was never really for him. [The 2002 Olympic disqualification] made Korean people feel politically weaker than Americans. He was in the middle of that."

That World Cup acceptance pleased Ohno. "I was really happy with the crowd's reaction. It was pretty positive right from the time we landed. Everything went really smooth. We were happy." It appeared that Koreans were warming up to a young man who had been so despised in their country. Several years later, during the 2010 Olympics in Vancouver, Korean skater Jung-Su Lee said, "Apolo has become the light of our sport. He is better known in Korea than the Korean skaters."

The flag of the Turin 2006 Winter Olympics

seven

A "Perfect" Run at the 2006 Olympics

Perfection is rarely achieved in sports, especially in such a high-powered competition as the Olympic Games. The few instances of perfection in sports include the occasional perfect game in bowling—twelve straight strikes—or the twenty-seven-up, twenty-seven-down excellence of a baseball pitcher's "perfect game."

But "perfect" was the word Apolo Ohno used to describe his gold medal-winning 500 meter race in the 2006 Olympics in Turin, Italy. A bit of perfection, and a dose of redemption as well. Ohno failed to make the finals in the 1500 meter. Koreans finished in first and second place in the 1500, gaining some revenge for Ohno's controversial win in that race in the 2002 Games.

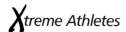

Ohno finished third behind two Korean skaters in the 1000. After those two races, fans were wondering if Ohno would win a gold medal. In the 500, however, everything went Ohno's way. After the race had been restarted twice by false starts, he timed the starter's gun perfectly and never trailed. No controversy in this one. Just dominance. Ohno said:

> I've been searching my entire career for the perfect race and that was it. I was in the moment at the time. I thought I timed the start just perfect. The starter had been pretty quick all day, so that's why there were so many false starts at the beginning. But that was really good for me.

Apolo Ohno celebrates winning the gold medal in the men's 500 meter short track speed skating final at the 2006 Winter Olympic Games in Turin, Italy, in February 2006.

When an athlete gets into that "zone," there's a feeling that time is standing still. Ohno said that's what happened in his 500 meter race. "I was really concentrating on just skating. And I think that is why when I came across that [finish] line, you saw the look on my face . . . My helmet is tilted. I am like— you know, kind of freaking out because I really was almost in awe and disbelief."

When it was over, Ohno couldn't resist celebrating. Hands upraised, he gave a hearty shout—so loud his father could hear it from the stands. He hugged friends, family, and other well-wishers. Then he took

a lap around the track with an American flag. "It was electric. It was perfect—or, at that instant, given everything, it surely seemed as close to perfect as perfect could be."

Later in the evening, Ohno helped the American team take bronze in the 5000 meter relay by passing the Italian skater on the final lap. The Korean team took home the gold. After the relay, the Koreans and American embraced, seemingly ending any animosity for past grievances.

Ohno would always remember the 2006 Olympics as validation of his determination to give up a "normal" life to train so hard for his sport. "I'm 23 years old. I like to have a social life, and that's pretty much out the window when it comes to an Olympic year," he said. "The things you give up, this is the reason why. Everything goes into this."

Four years later, in an interview before the 2010 Olympics, Ohno still had vivid memories of how he felt during that "perfect" 500 meter gold medal effort. "I just had total control over the race. I was completely immersed, I was in the zone, my flow was going smoothly . . . I mean, that race is 40 seconds long, give or take a couple of seconds. But when I was out there, it felt like it was 40 minutes. Literally, everything slows down. And I have four guys behind me basically trying to eat me. It was an amazing, amazing experience." And don't count on him forgetting that feeling anytime soon. "Days like this," he said, "you hope it lasts an eternity."

Apolo Ohno's Philosophy Of Olympic Competition:

"Every Olympic athlete prepares differently. For me, I am 100 percent into the sport. And if I decide to really make a crucial career decision to say, 'This is something I want to do,' I want to leave no stone unturned in my preparation. I think that allows me to be able to go to a competition, finish the race and, regardless of the outcome, I am able to step off the ice, still hold my chin up high, proud and happy that I went out there and competed my best. It is not up to me whether I win or lose. Ultimately, this might not be my day. And it is that philosophy toward sports, something that I really truly live by. I am emotional. I want to win. I am hungry. I am a competitor. I have that fire. But deep down, I truly enjoy the art of competing so much more than the result." ∎

Apolo Ohno and Julianne Hough, his partner on ABC's *Dancing with the Stars*

eight

Dancing With the Stars

F ame of a different kind awaited Apolo Ohno after his success at the 2006 Olympics. This time it was for dancing as a contestant on television's *Dancing With the Stars* in 2007. Well-known athletes are a popular attraction on the program. They usually perform well because of their grace, balance, and body awareness. Ohno was no exception. And he was in it to win. As he had told his agent when the offer first came, "I cannot not win. You don't understand. My friends will never let me live it down."

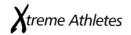

But he admitted being scared when the competition began. As confident as he was in an ice rink, he was not at all sure of himself on the dance floor. On the opening night of the series, when Ohno and partner Julianne Hough were given the "60 seconds to camera" warning, he totally forgot the music and the dance steps. "I had never, ever experienced that before a race," he said. "I had never blacked out. But this little dancing show—I was so nervous, so scared. I was dead-bang terrified. There were 25 to 30 million people about to watch me dance, live, on national television."

Partner Julianne Hough, an experienced dancer despite being only eighteen years old, helped Ohno get through that first dance, and for the next eight weeks they advanced through the popular show. When they scored well in the semifinals, it put them into the final night against pairs that included singer Joey Fatone and boxer Laila Ali.

The finals were held on March 22—Ohno's twenty-fifth birthday. He and Hough opened their final performance with a rumba to "Midnight Train to Georgia," then danced freestyle to "Bust a Move"—a routine that included some break dancing.

Their grand finale was a paso doble (a Latin-styled dance) to the Dario G's "Carnaval de Paris." Apolo wore a dark suit with a yellow bull logo on the back of the jacket and a yellow shirt. He began the dance by twirling Hough's skirt like a bullfighter. Then he draped it around her as they began the sensual, energetic performance that was a hit with the judges, who scored it three tens to win the competition. Judge Carrie Inaba was sold on Ohno's passion for the dancing. "I'm so excited to see Apolo win," she said. "He took it so seriously. He was the best technical dancer. He truly mastered the dances. Apolo and Julianne brought a whole new energy to the dance floor."

Romance?

As popular as Apolo Ohno has become, he has not been linked to a permanent female friend. He has said often that he won't be able to pursue a romance until his skating career is over and he has more time. "My girlfriend has been the ice," he once told an interviewer.

What would be the ideal girlfriend for the champion speed skater? In the summer of 2010 Ohno told *People* magazine he'd prefer his girlfriend not be a skater or a smoker, then added, "First and foremost, she has to have a good heart and good intentions. Those are key for me. A girl who appreciates trying new things is always great."

When might we see him with a special friend?

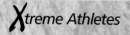

"I haven't found my lucky lady yet," he said during a busy schedule of promotional appearances. "It's very difficult to dedicate all of my time to someone like that when my life is like this. It would be unfair for both of us. I haven't closed the door on dating yet." ■

Apolo hoped his television fame would help raise awareness of speed skating. "In my sport performance is based on how I finish in the race, not how I 'wow' an audience. If I can emotionally pull the people watching into the dance, we have a winner! In a non-Olympic year, showcasing an Olympic athlete on a show that has millions of viewers—it's never heard of."

The big question was: would Apolo Ohno return to skating? The next Winter Olympics were a couple years away. The 2010 Games would be held in Vancouver, where Apolo had so much success as a youth. He hinted that these Games would be his final go-round as an Olympian. And he compared the Olympic experience with what he had just experienced on the dance floor. "The Games are sacrifice, heartbreak, drama—everything that reality shows try to capture. Maybe I should make my own reality show about that?"

Apolo Ohno at the premiere of *Pirates of the Caribbean 3* in 2007

The dancing experience had taught Ohno a few things about his ability to accept challenges outside of skating. "Being on that show opened up my heart. Many amateur athletes live inside this bubble and aren't really sociable. I was (sociable), but not until you got to know me. That show opened up my personality and allowed people to see who I was beneath the helmet, under the bandanna."

Soul Patch

Apolo Ohno is often identified by the distinctive "soul patch" on his chin. The soul patch is a growth of hair on a man's face, below the lip and above the chin—usually, when a man has no other facial hair on his chin.

The term came into being in the 1950s and '60s when the patch became popular with beatniks and jazz musicians. American trumpeter Dizzy Gillespie was one of the prominent musicians to grow one. But some historians point to such earlier "soul patch" wearers as William Shakespeare and Vlad the Impaler. Well-known men who have grown soul patches include musicians Ray Charles, Frank Zappa, Bruce Springsteen, and Stevie Wonder, actor Keanu Reeves, and Los Angeles Lakers coach Phil Jackson. In February of 2010, Alaska Airlines handed out fake "soul patches" to its customers at Sea-Tac Airport. The airline did the promotion because it was sponsoring Ohno in the Vancouver Olympics. ■

nine
A Lean Machine

In the years between the 2006 and 2010 Olympics, the question persisted: would Apolo Ohno answer the call of Hollywood or return for a third run at the Games? His experience on *Dancing With the Stars* had opened up his personality to the world. He had expressed a desire to try his hand in the entertainment industry, and word on the street was that he was discussing a movie role. He could retire at the top of his game, owning five Olympic medals. But Ohno had always said the medals were not his ultimate motivation. To carry on for one more

American Idol Jordin Sparks (left) and
Apolo Ohno at the Teen Choice Awards
in Universal City, California, in 2007

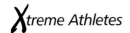

Olympics, it would have to be for the love of the sport. The love he rediscovered during that cold, wet winter's stay at Iron Springs. "I loved the sport when I was a teenager and I'd had to decide on the rocky shoreline of Western Washington whether I was going to be all in, and I loved it still."

Ohno believes the old saying that the journey is the destination. His skating journey had begun in Vancouver, where he had built his skills as a child. It had continued in Salt Lake City—his first Olympic experience. Now he lived in Salt Lake City, the new home of U.S. Speedskating, with the chance to come full circle back to Vancouver for the 2010 Games. So Hollywood would have to wait. The opportunity to skate in the Olympics in Vancouver was too attractive to turn down. Ohno said:

> My body is still healthy. I'm still young enough. If I go into directing, producing, acting—whatever it is in the entertainment world—those opportunities will be there when I'm done skating. At this point in my life I want to focus on things that are important to me. I won't be skating five or 10 years from now.

A key factor in Ohno's decision was the memories of all the drives with his father from Seattle to Vancouver to train as a boy. "This is very special.

It's special for my father, for all of my friends who are going to be there."

In 2008, Ohno proved he still had the fire, and the skills, by winning his first overall title at the world championships in Gangneung, South Korea. He fell to fifth in the 2009 worlds, but at the Olympic trials in Marquette, Michigan, in September he responded by winning the 500 and 1000.

Ohno would be twenty-seven at the Vancouver Olympics. He knew he needed to be in prime condition if he wanted to compete against the best skaters in the world. So many of them were much younger and lighter than him. So Ohno set out to get into the best shape of his life. The skater who once had been nicknamed "Chunky" began by slimming down from the 165 pounds he weighed in the 2002 and 2006 games.

Strength and conditioning coach John Schaeffer moved into Ohno's home in Salt Lake City. Schaeffer also trains NFL football players and mixed martial arts fighters. He and Ohno had been working together since before the 2006 Olympics. But in the months leading to the Vancouver Games, Schaeffer put Ohno through the most rigorous training program of all.

The goal was to get stronger and leaner. "This is going to be hell," Schaeffer told Ohno. "But in the end you're going to be the last man standing." Schaeffer gave Ohno this motivational slogan: "To accomplish

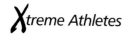

your goal, you have to be willing to sacrifice beyond what others are willing to sacrifice; you have to be willing to train at levels others are not willing to train at; you have to be willing to accept accomplishing goals that others never reach."

Through a combination of weights, running/cycling, saunas, and nutrition, Ohno was training like this could be his final Olympic go-round. He said:

> I love it that I've been here this long and I'm still very competitive. I take a lot of pride in that because our sport has such a high turnover. If this is the last hurrah, I want to make sure I have no regrets and there's nothing more I could have done. Right now my body feels so absolutely, unbelievably well. I wish I felt this good 10 years ago. If I'd known this before 2002, it would have been lights out.

Ohno ate mostly fish and vegetables and ran ten miles daily. He watched videos of his past races, had no phone calls after 6 p.m., no computer use after 7 p.m., and lights out at 9 p.m. "I put him through stuff he's never been through before," Schaeffer said. "He's stronger now than he has been. He's about as gifted an athlete as I've ever worked with." And lighter by twenty pounds. "I'm 145 and about two and a half percent body fat," Ohno said. "But I'm lifting more weight —actually, about double—than I was before the World Cups about three months ago."

The leaner, lighter, stronger Ohno was embracing his sport. "I love what I'm doing, more than I ever have in the past. I really do. This sport has not gotten any easier for me. In fact, it's gotten harder. But I love it." All that training paid off, Ohno said. "There's one thing for sure. Come these games, there's no one who's going to be fitter than me. There's just no way. Whether I can put it together on the ice or not and feel good, that's a different story. But I know, from a physical training standpoint, nobody's even close."

An interior and front exterior view of the Richmond Olympic Oval during the Vancouver 2010 Olympics

Richmond Olympic Oval
6111 River Road

ten

Back to Vancouver

By the time the 2010 Olympic Games arrived, Apolo Ohno was a superstar—a rare feat for a speed skater. As a twenty-seven-year-old veteran, the talk was now of his legacy—how many Olympic medals he could collect. The setting was perfect: Vancouver, where his skating career had taken off as a teenager. His role as an "elder statesman" of the U.S. team became clear when his practice skates in Vancouver took him past coaches who had once been his competitors. He said, "I'm like, 'I skated against you, you, you, you.' I skated against all these guys and now they're coaching athletes to beat me."

Ohno knew that it would be a challenge, and he was ready. "I'm more prepared for this than I've been for anything in my life. I'm in the best shape of my life, physically and mentally. I'm testing myself, seeing what

I still have inside. I'm where I want to be. My mind's in a very good place. It feels good to have my mojo back."

Yuki Ohno also believed his son would shine on familiar ice. "I have a vision. Apolo will entertain the world with an unbelievable performance. The battle is just getting started." But these Olympics would be more than just a homecoming for Ohno. He was chasing a record—Bonnie Blair's six Olympic medals, the most ever won by a U.S. Winter Olympian. It didn't take long for Ohno to catch Blair. By finishing second to South Korea's Jung-Su Lee in the 1500 meter short track race, Apolo became the most decorated short track skater in Olympic history with six medals in three Games. That silver medal also tied Blair, who earned her medals in long track skating in 1988, 1992, and 1994.

Ohno's silver in the 1500 meter was helped by a bit of misfortune by the South Koreans. They were one lap away from a 1-2-3 sweep when Si-Bak Sung and Ho-Suk Lee collided and crashed into the boards around the final turn. Ohno managed to avoid the crash. "Pretty intense," Ohno said after that race. "That's what the sport is all about. I skated a very aggressive race. I was battling with some of the best skaters in the world and it was a crazy race. I saw Ho-Suk set up a pretty wild pass. It did not work out well for him."

Ohno didn't consider himself merely a survivor, however. He insisted his silver was earned because he had come back from being slowed down with two laps to go by Sung. "I felt a Korean hand on my leg and I just lost a ton of speed. But it's the name of the game. Short track is one of the craziest events. It was a very, very aggressive race from the beginning and with a lap to go I lost a lot of speed but I skated a very, very hard race, I gave my all and I was awarded a silver medal."

The winner, Jung-Su Lee, revived the "Korea vs. Ohno" rift when he told a Korean news agency that Ohno's skating was "too aggressive." "Ohno didn't deserve to stand on the same medal platform with me," Lee said. "I was so enraged that it was hard for me to contain myself during the victory ceremony." J. R. Celski, a Federal Way native who began speed skating after watching Ohno in 2002, finished third.

Still to come was the 1000 meter and 500 meter races and the 5000 meter relay. Ohno declared he was not yet finished. "I do this sport because I love to compete and love what I'm doing," he said. "It's a fantastic start for the Olympic Games, but I still have a lot of heart left. Now I have six medals, I just feel good. It's like my first Olympics."

He knew his experience and conditioning were his edge in the upcoming races. "I've proved the power that I've brought to these games. I've proved my strength and that I'm a much different skater than in the past. I think that created some of the fear and confusion in the final—[my rivals] know I'm stronger. I have more events to compete in here, and I think I have an incredible opportunity that I could medal in three more."

A few days later Ohno passed Blair by taking bronze in the 1000 meter, finishing behind Jung-Su Lee and Ho-Suk Lee. His Olympic medal haul now included two gold, two silver, and three bronze. He accomplished that seventh medal with a full-out sprint from the back of the pack. He had slipped going around a turn with two laps to go, falling from second to last in the five-man race.

But his experience told Ohno that he was not finished. He passed the Canadian brothers Charles and Francois Hamelin to earn a spot at the podium—bronze, not gold, but still the record-setting seventh medal. Ohno said:

> Just one little mistake—I slipped. That's how crazy this sport is—one mistake. For anyone who might doubt that third place could feel great, this race was proof. This was one of my best races, ever. When all seemed lost, I thought, 'No, that is not going to happen. I am in this all the way to the end. I am going to fight.'"

He saw the race as a learning experience for the next generation of skaters. "Hopefully, kids who watch can take a lesson from that. That's the reason why you should never give up." There would be no eighth medal in the 500 meter, however. As Ohno charged from the back of the pack, he brushed against Canadian skater Francois-Louis Tremblay around the final turn. That sent Tremblay into the sideboards. Korean skater Sung also fell, bumping Canada's Charles Hamelin on the way down. Ohno crossed the finish line in second place behind a stumbling Hamelin, but was disqualified for bumping Tremblay.

Ohno admitted putting his hand out and touching Tremblay for protection. He explained that in the tightness of a short track race, trying to pass, there was just no room. "There was no space to move up. I kept waiting and waiting and on the last corner I ran up on the Canadian guy. I put my hand up so I wouldn't run into him. There was just no space."

Apolo Ohno (right), Canada's Charles Hamelin (center), and South Korea's Si-Bak Sung (left) compete during the second race of the men's 1000 meter short track skating semifinals competition at the Vancouver 2010 Olympics.

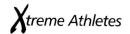

At first Ohno was quick to say that the judge that disqualified him was Canadian and the decision benefited Canadian skaters. But later he softened his tone. "I thought I had the silver," he said. "The judge saw something we didn't see . . . nothing like they were saying. It doesn't matter what I think. It's out of my control."

But Apolo Ohno had proved through the years that setbacks do not deter him. Since that fateful visit to the stormy Pacific coast in 1998, his determination has not waned. He showed his resilience once again in the 5000 meter relay. The disqualification in the 500 meter had fired him up, and he used that fire to help earn bronze for the United States. With his eighth medal in hand, Ohno praised his teammates. "There is nothing more I'd rather do than win a medal with these guys. They just skated their hearts out. Every one of them put their heart and soul into this. Some have had setbacks, struggles, that's life. This group of guys is very young and very talented. And the nice thing about an Olympic medal is that it is for life—it never goes away."

After the final race, one of Apolo's longtime foes saluted him. "We have some good memories and we also have some bad memories of Ohno," said Korean Ho-Suk Lee. "I will be sorry to see him leave the world of short track when he does." Ohno was able to see the big picture. "Regardless of whether I won gold, silver or bronze . . . I've come completely full circle in Vancouver."

Yuki Ohno had come full circle, too. All those days on the road, the youthful rebellion, and uncertainty of his early years: it all had come together. "His emotions are tighter right now than mine," Ohno said. "When I first started to learn how to speed-skate, he was there with me, when we went from Seattle to Vancouver to watch these Canadian skaters. It's amazing that we would make that trek when I was a kid who had a lot of energy and was out of control. I'm lucky to have him in my life."

Gold medalist Jung-Su Lee of South Korea (center), silver medalist Apolo Ohno (left), and bronze medalist J. R. Celski of the United States (right) pose on the podium during the medals ceremony of the men's 1500 meter short track skating finals competition at the Vancouver 2010 Olympics.

Apolo Ohno promoting The Century Council's "Ask, Listen, Learn"
program and his Apolo Anton Ohno Foundation, which encourages
kids to say "yes" to a healthy lifestyle and "no" to underage drinking

eleven

Life After the Olympics

If 2010 was Apolo Ohno's final go-round as an Olympian, his future still shines brightly. Although short track skating has been his life's calling and full-time occupation, Ohno also has given to society in charitable ventures.

During his time at the Olympic Training Center in Colorado Springs, Ohno studied business at the University of Colorado. He believes his success is due to healthy nutrition, which motivated him and

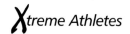

training coach John Schaeffer to develop a nutritional supplement business called 8 Zone. Ohno said he would love for 8 Zone to be a sponsor of future Olympic Games.

He also created the Apolo Anton Ohno Foundation and joined a national campaign to promote healthier lifestyles and to discourage teenagers from drinking alcohol. Ohno has been involved in campaigns to halt the spread of AIDS and other diseases in Africa and has helped the Salvation Army in clothing drives. He has helped raise money for the Ronald McDonald House in Seattle and for Nikkei Concerns, which provides care and services to Japanese people living in the Pacific Northwest.

Unlike professional athletes who earn money from their sport, Ohno and other winter-sports athletes rely on sponsorships for their finances. Because of his success and fame, Ohno has been sponsored by such corporations as McDonald's, General Electric, Vicks, Coca Cola, and Alaska Airlines—which put his image on the side of a jet.

Ohno took time off from his sport after the Vancouver Olympics. During a public appearance in California in November of 2010, he was asked when he might return to competitive skating. "Not in the next year," he replied. "I'm taking a long break." He said a lot of his time was concentrated on "things I've always wanted to do but just haven't had the time to do when I was an athlete," such as spending time on his foundation and looking into movie projects.

Ohno also spent a lot of time on the road. His post-Olympics schedule included a visit to a children's hospital, throwing out the first pitch at a Seattle Mariners baseball game, and touring to promote his latest autobiography.

He claims he's ready for the 2014 Games in Sochi, Japan—but maybe not as a competitor. If he does return to the ice for the 2014 Winter Olympics, would there be a danger that he would not be able to live up to previous achievements? Apolo said he's not concerned with that:

> An athlete chooses to compete for his or her own personal reasons. People aren't going to take away gold medals if you go to the next one and don't win a medal. Your results always stay with you. The one thing they say about an Olympic athlete is, 'Once an Olympian, always an Olympian.' So, that rings true with me. If I decided that it was the right decision for me to compete, and I had my own reasons for doing so . . . regardless of outcome, as long as I can get off the ice and I have no regrets about what I've done and my preparation, there's no shame.

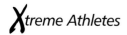

It's not just about winning, Apolo said. "To be honest with you, I could have walked away from the sport in 2006, when I had won my fifth medal," he said. "But I've always competed for, I think, reasons beyond just trying to reach the podium. More for internal, self-excellence . . . life lessons. I've been very lucky and very blessed to be healthy and have such a good and long career. But, we'll see. If my heart is still in it and wants to compete, then obviously I'll be back. And I will do it to the capacity that I think is necessary. But if not, I had a great run."

And the memories will not be of fame and acclaim. "When I'm done skating, I guarantee you I will not look back and remember standing on the podium," he said before the start of the Vancouver Olympics. "I'm going to remember . . . being with the team. Training alone, in my basement. Training when everybody else is sleeping. Doing things that nobody else is doing. Digging down, seeing what kind of character I really have. I love that stuff."

Yuki Ohno also understands the end of skating means the beginning of another venture in the partnership with his record-breaking son. During the Olympics in Vancouver, Yuki pondered the end of Apolo's career:

> Maybe we'll go back to a normal life. But life is never like that. New challenges, new things.

Because you're evolving. At least we won't be at the top of the mountain, feeling like we're going to be killed, or having to survive. We're inside the rink. We're fighting. We're chasing. That will end, but there will be something else.

When Apolo Ohno jets around the world in a life that might or might not still include skating, he understands how that life was shaped by a father who guided and supported him all the way. "I have certain times that I have to say to myself, I'm on a plane or I'm in a hotel room and I think, like 'Wow.' You're very grateful—you know, that I was blessed to have such a great dad."

Apolo Ohno talks to Hoda Kotb (left) and Kathie Lee Gifford (right) on NBC News's *Today* show.

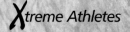

A World-Class Career

Here is a list of medals an honors won
by Apolo Ohno in major skating competitions:

Olympics
Vancouver 2010: Silver in 1500m; bronze in 1000m;
  bronze in 5000m relay.
Turin 2006: Gold in 500m; bronze in 1000m; bronze
  in 5000m relay.
Salt Lake City 2002: Gold in 1500m; silver in 1000m.

World Cup
Three-time World Cup overall champion (2001,
  2003, 2005).
Seven-time World Cup event champion.

World Championships (2001-09)
Nine gold, seven silver, seven bronze.

U.S. Championships
Seven-time short track overall champion (1997, 1999,
  2001-2005).

World Junior Championships
Montreal 1999: Gold in 1000m; gold in super 1500m;
  overall gold.

Medal Count

Olympics

Gold: 2002 Salt Lake City 1500m; 2006 Turin 500m.

Silver: 2002 Salt Lake City 1000m; 2010 Vancouver 1500m.

Bronze: 2006 Turin 1000m; 2006 Turin 5000m relay; 2010 Vancouver 1000m; 2010 Vancouver 5000m relay.

World Championships

Gold: 2001 Jeonju, 1500m; 2001 Jeonju, 5000m relay; 2005 Beijing, 1000m; 2005 Beijing, 3000m; 2007 Milan, 1500m; 2008, Gangneung, overall; 2008 Gangneung, 500m; 2008 Harbin, Team; 2009 Vienna, 5000m relay.

Silver: 1999 Sofia, 500m; 2001 Jeonju, Overall; 2001 Jeonju, 1000m; 2003 Warsaw, 3000m; 2005 Beijing, Overall; 2008 Gangneung, 1000m; 2009, Vienna, 1000m.

Bronze: 2005 Beijing, 5000m relay; 2007 Milan, Overall; 2007 Milan, 1000m; 2007 Milan, 3000m; 2007 Milan, 5000m relay; 2008 Gangneung, 3000m; 2009 Heerenveen, Team. ■

Timeline

1982 Born on May 22 in Seattle, Washington, to Yuki Ohno and Jerrie Lee.

1983 Mother, Jerrie Lee, leaves the family; parents divorce.

1994 Wins breaststroke at Washington State Junior Swimming Championship; watches Winter Olympics in Lillehammer, Norway, and becomes hooked on speed skating.

1996 Admitted into Lake Placid Olympic Training center; at fourteen, youngest skater ever admitted.

1997 Wins overall title at U.S. Seniors Championships (first of seven), youngest skater ever to earn that title.

1998 Finishes last in U.S. Olympic trials.

1999 Wins overall title at World Junior Championship; fourth overall at World Championships.

2001 World Cup overall champion; second overall at World Championships.

2002 Wins gold in 1500 meter and silver in 1000 meter his first Olympic Games in Salt Lake City.

2003 Wins World Cup overall title for second time.

2005 Wins gold in 1000 meters and 3000 meters at World Championships in Beijing; wins overall at World Cup for third time.

2006 Wins three medals at Olympics in Turin, Italy, (gold in the 500 meters, bronze in the 1000 meters, bronze in the 5000 meters relay).

2007 Wins television's *Dancing With the Stars,* with partner Julianne Hough.

2008 Wins World Championships overall title for the first time at Gangneung, South Korea.

2010 In his return to Vancouver, where he skated often as a youth, wins three medals (silver in the 1500 meters, bronze in the 1000 meters and 5000 meters relay) for a career-record eight, breaking Bonnie Blair's record.

Sources

Chapter One: The Cold, Wet Truth

pp.12-13, "You have to . . ." Ron Claiborne, "Apolo Ohno Has a Single Father Behind His Success," *ABC News,* June 18, 2006.

p. 13, "I want . . ." Apolo Ohno and Nancy Richardson, *A Journey: the Autobiography of Apolo Anton Ohno* (New York: Simon & Schuster Books for Young Readers, 2002), 62.

p. 13, "My father . . ." Ibid., 11.

Chapter Two: Watch Out, Here He Comes

pp. 15-16,"They expected me . . ." Elliott Almond, "Apolo Ohno: Completing a Family Circle," *Seattle Times,* January 15, 1998.

pp. 16-17, "Because I was so young . . ." Apolo Ohno, *Zero Regrets: Be Better Than Yesterday* (New York: Atria Books, 2010), 11.

p. 17, "My father and I . . ." Ohno and Richardson, *A Journey: the Autobiography of Apolo Anton Ohno,* 13-14.

p. 17, "I don't have any . . ." Gary Shelton, "Ohno's Ups and Downs," *St. Petersburg Times,* February 17, 2003.

p. 18, "To be honest . . ." Interview by Billy Bush, "Apolo Anton Ohno Talks Love Life, Olympic Future & Questions Surrounding His Mother," *Access Hollywood,* February 24, 2010.

p. 18, "Everything changed . . ." S. L. Price, "Launch of Apolo," *Sports Illustrated,* February 14, 2002.

p. 18, "Can I do this? . . ." Claiborne, "Apolo Ohno Has a Single Father Behind His Success."

p. 18, "I was a quick ..." Ohno and Richardson, *A Journey: the Autobiography of Apolo Anton Ohno,* 17.

p. 18, "My dad figured . . ." Ibid.

pp. 19-20, "In the beginning . . ." Ibid., 15.

p. 20, "He saw something . . ." Claiborne, "Apolo Ohno Has a Single Father Behind His Success."

p. 20, "Surprisingly, I kept up . . ." Ohno and Richardson, *A Journey: the Autobiography of Apolo Anton Ohno,* 18.

p. 20, "I think there was . . ." Claiborne, "Apolo Has a Single Father Behind His Success."

p. 21,   "I had no doubt . . ." Craig Hill, "Ohno-Celski: The Veteran and the Comeback Kid," *Tacoma News-Tribune,* February 11, 2010.

p. 21,   "A few of my friends . . ." Ohno and Richardson, *A Journey: the Autobiography of Apolo Anton Ohno,* 42.

p. 21,   "One guy . . ." Price, "Launch of Apolo."

p. 21,   "Sports saved me . . ." Hill, "Ohno-Celski: The Veteran and the Comeback Kid."

p. 22,   "waterfront, lakes . . ." Official Web site of the City of Federal Way, http://www.cityoffederalway.com.

Chapter Three: Discovering the Ice

p. 27,   "I don't mind prioritizing . . ." Percy Allen, "Fed. Way Speedskater Decides Do Take His Time," *Seattle Times,* March 15, 1996.

p. 30,   "He had his . . ." Hill, "Ohno-Celski: The Veteran and the Comeback Kid."

p. 30,   "He was overprotective . . ." Almond, "Apolo Ohno: Completing a Family Circle."

p. 30,   "Chances don't come . . ." Ohno and Richardson, *A Journey: The Autobiography of Apolo Anton Ohno,* 32.

p. 31,   "Dad told me . . . " Price, "Launch of Apolo."

pp. 31-32, "Dad literally packed . . ." Ohno and Richardson, *A Journey: the Autobiography of Apolo Anton Ohno,* 33-34.

p. 32,   "As the days wore on . . ." Ibid., 34.

pp. 32-33, "Dad explained to me . . ." Ibid., 35-36.

p. 33,   "I escorted Apolo . . ." Almond, "Apolo Ohno: Completing a Family Circle."

p. 33,   "Good luck . . ." Hill, "Ohno-Celski: The Veteran and the Comeback Kid."

Chapter Four: Teenager On Top

p. 35,   "I hated it . . ." Price, "Launch of Apolo."

p. 35,   "I was a thick kid . . ." Steve Ginsburg, "Ohno Chooses Skating Over Hollywood, For Now," Reuters, February 16, 2009.

pp. 35-36, "I don't want . . ." Price, "Launch of Apolo."

p. 36,   "He totally changed . . ." Ibid.

p. 36,   "It has really helped him . . ." Almond, "Apolo Ohno: Completing a Family Circle."

pp. 36-37, "Instead of putting . . ." Ohno, *Zero Regrets: Be Better Than Yesterday*, 63

p. 37, "The whole season . . ." Hill, "Ohno-Celski: The Veteran and the Comeback Kid."

pp. 38-39, "Everything had changed . . ." Ohno and Richardson, *A Journey: the Autobiography of Apolo Anton Ohno*, 62.

p. 39, "He had always . . ." Ibid., 63.

Chapter Five: First Taste of Controversy

p. 45, "Reporters asked me . . ." Ohno and Richardson, *A Journey: the Autobiography of Apolo Anton Ohno*, 108.

p. 48, "I think Apolo . . ." Selena Roberts, "Fix Charge Is a Threat To Skater Ohno," *New York Times*, January 22, 2002.

pp. 48-49, "I went over . . ." Ohno and Richardson, *A Journey: the Autobiography of Apolo Anton Ohno*, 109.

p. 49, "Neither Ohno, Smith . . ." Ibid., 118-119.

Chapter Six: Apolo's First Olympics

p. 51, "It's a dying sport . . ." Price, "Launch of Apolo."

p. 53, "That was definitely . . ." Ohno, *Zero Regrets: Be Better Than Yesterday*, 137.

pp. 53-54, "I was tasting it . . ." Ibid.

p. 59, "I grew up around . . ." Karen Crouse, "Ohno is Hoping for Victories and Thaw in Icy Relations With South Koreans," *New York Times*, February 12, 2006.

pp. 60-61, "I went to . . ." Brian Cazeneuve, "Still On the Fast Track," *Sports Illustrated*, December 13, 2004.

p. 61, "I thought I was prepared . . ." Chris Jones, "One Thing Perfectly: Catching Up with Apolo Ohno," *Esquire Magazine*, February 1, 2006.

pp.61-62, "The entire Olympic experience . . ." Ohno, *Zero Regrets: Be Better Than Yesterday*, 155-156.

p. 62, "He won them over . . ." Brian Cazeneuve, "Apolo Still Has His Edge," *Sports Illustrated*, February 22, 2010.

p. 63, "I was really happy . . ." "Ex-villain Ohno Overjoyed with Korean Cheers," *AFP*, October 12, 2006.

p. 63, "Apolo has become . . ." Cazeneuve, "Apolo Still Has His Edge."

Chapter Seven: A "Perfect" Run at the 2006 Olympics

p. 66,   "I've been searching . . ." Bernie Wilson, "Oh, What a Night," *Yahoo Sports,* February 25, 2006.

p. 67,   "I was really concentrating . . ." Jaymie, "Olympic Speed Skater Apolo Anton Ohno," *Asiance Magazine,* January 31, 2010.

p. 68,   "It was electric . . ." Ohno, *Zero Regrets: Be Better Than Yesterday,* 191.

p. 68,   "I'm 23 years old . . ." Wilson, "Oh, What a Night."

p. 68,   "I just had total control . . ." Jaymie, "Olympic Speed Skater Apolo Anton Ohno."

p. 69,   "Days like this . . ." Wilson, "Oh, What a Night."

p. 69,   "Every Olympic athlete . . ." Jaymie, "Olympic Speed Skater Apolo Ohno."

Chapter Eight: Dancing With the Stars

p. 71,   "I cannot not win . . ." Ohno, *Zero Regrets: Be Better Than Yesterday,* 199.

p. 72,   "I had never, ever . . ." Ibid., 201.

p. 73,   "I'm so excited . . ." Monica Rizzo and Michelle Tan, "Apolo Anton Ohno Wins Dancing With the Stars," *People,* May 23, 2007.

pp. 73-74, "My girlfriend . . ." Kate Hallett, "Apolo Ohno's Perfect Woman Doesn't Have to Skate," *People*, August 14, 2010.

p. 73,   "First and foremost . . ." Ibid.

p. 74,   "I haven't found . . ." Ibid.

p. 74,   "In my sport . . ." Monica Rizzo, "Ohno A-Go-Go," *People,* April 30, 2007.

p. 74,   "The games are . . ." Ibid.

p. 76,   "Being on that show . . ." Jay Mariotti, "Apolo Ohno Has 'Mojo' Back, Might Conquer Games," *Olympics Fanhouse,* February 12, 2010.

Chapter Nine: A Lean Machine

p. 80,   "I loved the sport . . ." Ohno, *Zero Regrets: Be Better Than Yesterday,* 221.

p. 80,   "My body . . ." Ginsburg, "Ohno Chooses Skating Over Hollywood, For Now."

pp. 80-81, "This is very special . . ." Ron Judd, "Apolo Ohno Savors Final Chapter in Storied Olympics Career," *Seattle Times,* February 6, 2010.

p. 81, "This is going . . ." Ohno, *Zero Regrets: Be Better Than Yesterday,* 244.

pp. 81-82, "To accomplish..." Ibid., 246.

p. 82, "I love it . . ." Beth Harris, "Apolo Anton Ohno Remakes Himself for 3rd Olympics," Associated Press, February 24, 2010.

p. 82, "I put him through . . ." Ibid.

pp. 82-83, "I'm 145 and . . ." Kevin Woodley, "Ohno Lightens Up in Quest for Gold, Associated Press, February 9, 2010.

p. 83, "I love what I'm doing . . ." Judd, "Apolo Ohno Savors Final Chapter in Storied Olympics Career."

p. 83, "There's one thing . . ." Ibid.

Chapter Ten: Back to Vancouver

p. 85, "I'm like . . ." John Powers, "Mission Accomplished," *Boston Globe,* February 26, 2010.

pp. 85-86, "I'm more prepared . . ." Mariotti, "Apolo Ohno Has 'Mojo' Back, Might Conquer Games."

p. 86, "I have a vision . . ." Greg Bishop, "On and Off the Ice, Ohno Is Positioned for Success," *New York Times,* February 20, 2010.

p. 86, "Pretty intense ..." Mariotti, "Apolo Ohno Has 'Mojo' Back, Might Conquer Games."

pp. 86-87, "I felt a Korean hand . . ." Howard Bryant, "'Historic Night' for U.S. Speedskater," *ESPN,* February 14, 2010.

p. 87, "Ohno didn't deserve . . ." Ohno, *Zero Regrets: Be Better Than Yesterday,* 269.

p. 87, "I do this sport . . ." "I'm Just Warming Up, Says Record-setting Ohno," *AFP,* February 14, 2010.

p. 87, "I've proved . . ." Mariotti, "Apolo Ohno Has 'Mojo' Back, Might Conquer Games."

p. 88, "Just one little mistake . . ." Ohno, *Zero Regrets: Be Better Than Yesterday,* 273.

p. 89, "Hopefully, kids who watch . . ." Harris, "Apolo Ohno Remakes Himself for 3rd Olympics."

p. 89, "There was no space . . ." Filip Bondy, "Despite DQ, Two More Medals," *New York Daily News,* February 27, 2010.

p. 90,   "I thought I had . . ." Greg Bishop, "Disqualified in 500, Ohno Wins 8ᵗʰ Medal," *New York Times,* February 27, 2010.

p. 90,   "There is nothing more . . ." "Canada Wins 5,000 Relay Gold," February 26, 2010, www.vancouver.com.

p. 90,   "We have some . . ." Beth Harris, "Ohno Earns Bronze in Relay, DQ'd in 500 Final," Associated Press, February 27, 2010.

p. 90,   "Regardless of whether . . ." "I'm Just Warming Up, Says Record-setting Ohno."

p. 91,   "His emotions are tighter . . ." Mariotti, "Apolo Ohno Has 'Mojo' Back, Might Conquer Games."

Chapter Eleven: Life After the Olympics

p. 94,   "Not in the next year . . ." Apolo Ohno, book signing appearance, Barnes & Noble, Fresno, California, November 29, 2010.

pp. 94-95, "things I've always wanted . . ." Gregg Bell, "Ohno Happy Without Skating, Undecided on Return," Associated Press, June 23, 2010.

p. 95,   "An athlete chooses . . ."Alex Raskin, "Ohno in Sochi? Apolo Not Ready to Say Oh-no Yet," Red Line Editorial, July 26, 2010.

p. 96,   "To be honest with you," "Ohno on Possible Retirement: 'I Had a Great Run,'" Associated Press, June 24, 1010.

p. 96,   "When I'm done . . ." Judd, "Apolo Ohno Savors Final Chapter in Storied Olympics Career."

pp. 96-97, "Maybe we'll go back . . ." Bishop, "On and Off the Ice, Ohno Is Positioned for Success."

p. 97,   "I have certain . . ." Claiborne, "Apolo Ohno Has a Single Father Behind His Success."

Bibliography

Abrahamson, Alan. "With His Mojo, Ohno Makes History." *Universal Sports,* February 14, 2010.

Allen, Percy. "Fed. Way Speedskater Decides to Take His Time." *Seattle Times,* March 15, 1996.

Almond, Elliott. "Apolo Ohno: Completing A Family Circle." *Seattle Times,* January 15, 1998.

"Apolo Ohno's Mother Was Teenager When She Gave Birth To Future Olympian." *Asianista.com,* February 27, 2010.

Bell, Gregg. "Ohno Happy Without Skating, Undecided on Return." Associated Press, June 24, 2010.

Bishop, Greg. "Disqualified in 500, Ohno Wins 8th Medal." *New York Times,* February 27, 2010.

_____."On and Off the Ice, Ohno Is Positioned for Success." *New York Times,* February 20, 2010.

Cazenuuve, Brian. "Apollo Still Has His Edge." *Sports Illustrated,* February 22, 2010.

_____."Did They or Didn't They?" *Sports Illustrated,* February 13, 2002.

_____."Still On the Fast Track." *Sports Illustrated,* December 13, 2004.

Claiborne, Ron. "Apolo Ohno Had a Single Father Behind His Success." *ABC News,* June 18, 2006.

Crouse, Karen. "Ohno is Hoping for Victories and Thaw in Icy Relations With South Koreans." *New York Times,* February 12, 2006.

Ginsburg, Steve. "Ohno Chooses Skating Over Hollywood, for Now." Reuters. February 19, 2009.

Harris, Beth. "Apolo Anton Ohno Remakes Himself for 3rd Olympics." Associated Press, February 23, 2010.

Hollett, Kate. "Apolo Ohno's Perfect Woman Doesn't Have to Skate." *People,* August 14, 2010.

Jaymie. "Olympian Speed Skater Apolo Anton Ohno." *Asiance Magazine,* January 31, 2010.

Jones, Chris. "One Thing Perfectly: Catching up with Apolo

Ohno." *Esquire Magazine,* February, 2006.

Judd, Ron. "Apolo Ohno Savors Final Chapter in Storied Olympics Career." *Seattle Times,* February 7, 2010.

Mariotti, Jay. "Apolo Ohno Has 'Mojo' Back, Might Conquer Games." *Olympics Fanhouse,* February 14, 2010.

Ohno, Apolo. *Zero Regrets: Be Greater Than Yesterday.* New York: Atria Books, 2010.

———, and Nancy Richardson. *A Journey: The Autobiography of Apolo Anton Ohno.* New York: Simon Schuster Books for Young Readers, 2002.

"Olympian Speed Skater Apolo Anton Ohno." *Asiance Magazine,* January 31, 2010.

Price, S. L. "Launch of Apolo." *Sports Illustrated,* February 4, 2002.

Raskin, Alex. "Ohno in Sochi? Apolo Not Ready to Say Oh-no Yet." Red Line Editorial, July 26, 2010.

Rizzo, Monica, and Michelle Tan. "Apolo Anton Ohno Wins Dancing With the Stars." *People,* May 23, 2007.

Roberts, Selena. "Fix Charge is a Threat to Skater Ohno." *New York Times,* January 22, 2002.

Shelton, Gary. "Ohno's Ups and Downs." *St. Petersburg Times,* February 17, 2002.

Wilson, Bernie. "Oh, What a Night." *Yahoo Sports,* February 25, 2006.

Web sites

http://www.usspeedskating.org
Official site of U.S. Speedskating.

http://www.olympic.org
Official site of the Olympic Movement, with links to players
and sports.

http://www.worldshorttrack.com
A resource that provides news, information, and statistics about
short track speed skating around the world.

http://www.apoloantonohno.com
Ohno's official site.

http://www.gotapolo.com
Fan site devoted to the skater.

http://www.answers.com/topic/apolo-anton-ohno
An extensive biography of Ohno.

Index

Photo Credits